First Facts

First Cookbooks

An Astronaut COOKBOOK

Simple Recipes for Kids

by Sarah L. Schuette

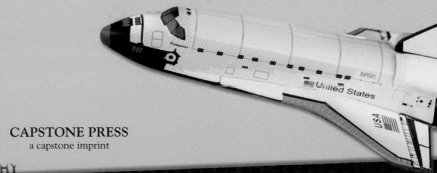

CAPSTONE PRESS
a capstone imprint

First Facts is published by Capstone Press,
151 Good Counsel Drive, P.O. Box 669, Mankato, Minnesota 56002.
www.capstonepub.com

 Books published by Capstone Press are manufactured with paper
containing at least 10 percent post-consumer waste.

Library of Congress Cataloging-in-Publication Data
Schuette, Sarah L., 1976–
  An astronaut cookbook : simple recipes for kids / by Sarah L. Schuette.
    p. cm.—(First facts. First cookbooks)
  Summary: "Provides instructions and close-up step photos for making a variety of simple snacks and
drinks with an astronaut theme"—Provided by publisher.
  Includes bibliographical references and index.
  ISBN 978-1-4296-5376-3 (library binding)
  1. Cooking—Juvenile literature. I. Title. II. Series.

TX652.5.S3435 2011
641.5'123—dc22

2010028141

Editorial Credits

Lori Shores, editor; Juliette Peters, designer; Sarah Schuette, photo stylist; Marcy Morin, studio scheduler;
    Laura Manthe, production specialist

Photo Credits

All photos by Capstone Studio/Karon Dubke except:
Getty Images Inc., 4 (bottom)

The author dedicates this book in memory of her grandmother, Minnie Simcox.

Printed in the United States of America in North Mankato, Minnesota.
092010
005933CGS11

Table of Contents

Introduction: Out of this World Good 4

Tools 6

Techniques 7

Shooting Stars 8   Flying Saucers 10

Moon Rock Salad 12   Comet Crunch.................... 14   The Big Dipper................. 16

Astronaut Ice Cream......... 18   Saturn's Rings.................... 20

Glossary 22

Read More 23

Internet Sites 23

Index 24

Out of this World Good

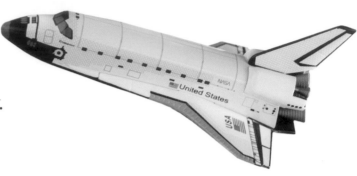

Blast off into the kitchen to whip up some **universal** treats. They're great for after school snacks or a space-themed party.

First you'll need to go over your flight plan. Read each recipe. Then look in your kitchen for the tools and **ingredients** you'll need. Have any questions? Ask an adult.

Before you begin, **dock** your shuttle at the sink, and wash your hands. Put on an apron, and be sure to clean up after yourself. **Astronauts** always keep the space station clean.

Metric Conversion Chart	
United States	**Metric**
¼ teaspoon	1.2 mL
½ teaspoon	2.5 mL
1 teaspoon	5 mL
1 tablespoon	15 mL
¼ cup	60 mL
⅓ cup	80 mL
½ cup	120 mL
⅔ cup	160 mL
¾ cup	175 mL
1 cup	240 mL
1 ounce	30 gms

5

Tools

Think of your kitchen as mission control. It's the command post for everything you need to get cooking. Use this guide to choose the right stuff.

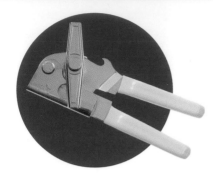

can opener—a tool used to open metal cans

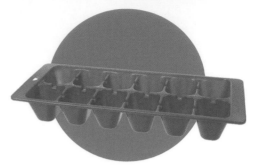

cookie cutter—a hollow shape made from metal or plastic that is used to cut cookie dough

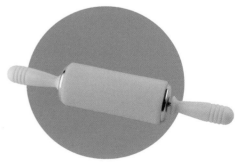

ice cube tray—a sectioned tray made of plastic used to freeze water into cube shapes

liquid measuring cup—a glass or plastic measuring cup with a spout for pouring

measuring cups—round, flat cups with handles used for measuring dry ingredients

measuring spoons—spoons with small deep scoops used to measure both wet and dry ingredients

mixing bowl—a sturdy bowl used for mixing ingredients

oven mitt—a large mitten made from heavy fabric used to protect hands when removing hot pans from the oven

rolling pin—a kitchen tool shaped like a cylinder that is used to flatten dough or crush ingredients

rubber scraper—a kitchen tool with a rubber paddle on one end

strainer—a bowl-shaped tool with holes in the sides and bottom used for draining liquid off food

Techniques

crush—to squash something under a heavy weight

drain—to remove the liquid from something

fold—to mix ingredients gently by lifting a mixture up and over itself

measure—to take a specific amount of something

spread—to cover a surface with something

stir—to mix something by moving a spoon around in it

Shooting Stars

There are millions of stars in the sky. There are also a million ways to make a sandwich. Try this one first. Then **invent** one of your own.

Makes 1 sandwich

Ingredients:
- 2 slices whole wheat bread
- 1 teaspoon honey mustard dressing
- 1 leaf iceberg lettuce
- 2 slices shaved turkey
- 1 slice Swiss cheese

Tools:
- plate
- measuring spoons
- 3-inch star cookie cutter

1 Place one slice of bread on a plate.

2 Measure 1 teaspoon honey mustard dressing. Use the measuring spoon to spread the dressing on the bread.

3 Lay a piece of lettuce on top of the dressing.

4 Add turkey slices and Swiss cheese.

5 Top with another piece of bread.

6 Press down on a cookie cutter to cut out a star shape. Eat the star now, and save the rest of the sandwich for later.

Flying Saucers

Do you believe in space aliens? What about **UFOs**? Crunch on this yummy flying saucer while you decide.

Makes 1 saucer

Ingredients:
- 1 rice cake
- 1 tablespoon pizza sauce
- ⅛ cup shredded mozzarella cheese
- 8 slices mini turkey pepperoni

Tools:
- plate
- measuring spoons
- measuring cups

1 Lay a rice cake on a plate.

2 Measure and add 1 tablespoon of pizza sauce.

3 Use the measuring spoon to spread the sauce on the rice cake.

4 Measure and add cheese.

5 Place pepperoni slices on top of cheese.

TIP You can also add other pizza ingredients that you like.

11

Moon Rock Salad

When astronauts landed on the moon in 1969, they collected moon rocks. But they never found any rocks as sweet as these. This fruit salad only looks like moon rocks.

Makes 4 servings

Ingredients:
- 1 bunch grapes, washed
- 1 12-ounce can fruit cocktail
- 1 12-ounce can mandarin oranges
- 1 cup mini marshmallows
- 4 snack size tapioca pudding cups

Tools:
- mixing bowl
- can opener
- strainer
- measuring cups
- rubber scraper

1 Remove grapes from their stems. Place grapes into a mixing bowl.

2 Have an adult open the cans of fruit. Use a strainer to drain the liquid. Add fruit to the bowl.

3 Measure and add marshmallows to the fruit.

4 Empty the pudding cups into the bowl.

5 Use a rubber scraper to fold mixture together.

TIP Add some chopped pecans to add a little crunch to this fruit salad.

Comet Crunch

Comets are made of chunks of dust, ice, and rock. Yuck! Luckily, this snack mix is made of tastier stuff.

Makes 2 servings

Ingredients:
- 1 cup round cereal pieces
- 1 cup small pretzels
- ½ cup yogurt covered raisins
- ½ cup dried cranberries
- ½ cup peanuts

Tools:
- measuring cups
- 1-gallon zip-top plastic bag

1 Measure cereal and pretzels. Put them in a zip-top plastic bag.

2 Measure and add ½ cup each of raisins, cranberries, and peanuts.

3 Close the plastic bag tightly. Shake the bag gently to mix the ingredients.

TIP You can also add candy or dried fruit to the mix.

The Big Dipper

People have told stories about the stars for years. The Big Dipper is one of the most famous **constellations** in the night sky. This dip is so delicious, you'll be talking about it for years!

Makes 6 servings

Ingredients:

- 1 8-ounce container light sour cream
- 1 package dry ranch dressing mix
- 1 tablespoon milk
- baby carrots
- celery sticks

Tools:

- mixing bowl
- spoon
- measuring spoons

1 Empty the container of sour cream into a mixing bowl.

2 Use a spoon to stir in dry ranch dressing mix.

3 Measure and add milk to the bowl. Stir again.

4 Serve dip with baby carrots and celery sticks.

Astronaut Ice Cream

Space shuttles rattle and shake as they blast off. Pretend you're on a space shuttle. Grab a fellow astronaut and take turns shaking up some ice cream.

Makes 1 serving

Ingredients:
- 2 tablespoons sugar
- 1 cup heavy cream
- ½ teaspoon vanilla extract
- 2 trays of ice cubes
- ½ cup rock salt

Tools:
- measuring spoons
- 1-pint zip-top plastic bag
- liquid measuring cup
- 1-gallon zip-top freezer bag
- oven mitts

TIP Mix in your favorite fruit pieces after shaking.

1 Measure sugar and place in a 1-pint zip-top plastic bag.

2 Measure and add cream and vanilla to the bag. Seal the bag completely.

3 Place ice cubes in a 1-gallon zip-top freezer bag. Measure rock salt and add to the bag.

4 Place the 1-pint bag in the 1-gallon freezer bag. Seal the larger bag.

5 Put on oven mitts. Shake the bag for five minutes.

6 Remove the smaller bag and enjoy your ice cream.

Saturn's Rings

The rings around Saturn are made of ice chunks! Make your own drinks with colorful icy rings. You don't even need to leave Earth to do it. **Makes 2 drinks**

Ingredients:
- 4 single serving containers of sport drinks in different colors

Tools:
- liquid measuring cup
- 2 ice cube trays
- 4 zip-top plastic bags
- rolling pin
- spoon
- 2 glasses

1 Pour one sport drink into a liquid measuring cup. Use the measuring cup to fill four ice cube tray spaces. Repeat with other sport drinks.

2 Put the ice cube trays in the freezer overnight.

3 Pop colored drink cubes out of the trays. Put each color of cube into its own zip-top plastic bag.

4 Crush the ice in each bag with a rolling pin.

5 Use a spoon to layer the crushed ice into two glasses.

TIP You can use fruit juice for this recipe too.

Glossary

astronaut (ASS-truh-nawt)—a person who is trained to live and work in space

comet (KOM-it)—a ball of rock and ice that circles the Sun

constellation (kahn-stuh-LAY-shuhn)—a group of stars that forms a shape

dock (DOK)—to join with a space station or another space craft in space

ingredient (in-GREE-dee-uhnt)—an item used to make something else

invent (in-VENT)—to create a new thing or method

UFO (YOO EF OH)—an object in the sky thought to be a spaceship from another planet; UFO is short for Unidentified Flying Object

universal (yoo-nuh-VUR-suhl)—shared by everyone or everything

Read More

Fauchald, Nick. *Holy Guacamole!: and other Scrumptious Snacks.* Kids Dish. Minneapolis: Picture Window Books, 2008.

Wilkes, Angela. *First Cooking Activity Book.* London: Dorling Kindersley, 2008.

Internet Sites

FactHound offers a safe, fun way to find Internet sites related to this book. All of the sites on FactHound have been researched by our staff.

Here's all you do:

Visit *www.facthound.com*

Type in this code: 9781429653763

Super-cool stuff!

Check out projects, games and lots more at
www.capstonekids.com

Index

Astronaut Ice Cream, 18–19
astronauts, 4, 12, 18

The Big Dipper, 16–17

cleaning, 4
Comet Crunch, 14–15
comets, 14
constellations, 16

Flying Saucers, 10–11

ingredients, 4

metric guide, 4
Moon Rock Salad, 12–13

safety, 13
Saturn's Rings, 20–21
Shooting Stars, 8–9
space shuttle, 18
stars, 8, 16

techniques, 7
tools, 4, 6–7

UFOs, 10